Founder's Pocket
Term Sheets
and
Preferred Shares

1x1MEDIA

Simple, quick answers, all in one place.

By

Stephen R. Poland

1x1 Media
Asheville, North Carolina
United States

Care has been taken to verify the accuracy of information in this book. However, the authors and publisher cannot accept responsibility for consequences from application of the information in this book, and makes no warranty, expressed or implied, with respect to its content.

Trademarks: Some of the product names and company names included in this book have been used for identification purposes only and may be trademarks or registered trade names of their respective manufacturers and sellers. The author and publisher disclaim any affiliation, association, or connection with, or sponsorship or endorsement by, such owners.

ISBN 978-1-938162-06-0

©2016 by 1x1 Media, LLC

email: info@1x1media.com

website : www.1x1media.com

Table of Contents

Founder's Pocket Guide: Term Sheets & Preferred Shares

"Timing, perseverance, and ten years of trying will eventually make you look like an overnight success."

- Biz Stone, Twitter co-founder

What the Founder's Pocket Guide Series Delivers

We developed the *Founder's Pocket Guide* series to provide quick answers to common questions encountered by entrepreneurs. Consider the following dilemmas:

> "I sort of know **what startup equity is**, but really don't understand the details, and I have an investor interested in my company. Where do I start?"

> "My co-founder said we need to **build a cap table to track our equity ownership**—how do we get started?"

> "My co-founders and I need to determine **how to divide the ownership** of our startup, but how can we be certain we get it right?"

> "I've heard that **convertible debt is a good funding structure for early-stage startups**. What is convertible debt and how do I approach potential investors with a funding pitch?"

The *Founder's Pocket Guide* series addresses each of the topics in a concise and easy to reference format.

Look for these current titles at www.1x1media.com:

- *Founder's Pocket Guide: Founder Equity Splits*
- *Founder's Pocket Guide: Cap Tables*
- *Founder's Pocket Guide: Convertible Debt*
- *Founder's Pocket Guide: Startup Valuation*
- *Founder's Pocket Guide: Friends & Family Funding*

Disclaimers

The content in this guide is not intended as legal, financial, or tax advice and cannot be relied upon for any purpose without the services of a qualified professional. With that disclaimer in mind, here's our position on how to best use the guidance provided in this work.

Great entrepreneurs use all the resources available to them, making the best decisions they can to mitigate risk and yet move ahead with the most important tasks in their roadmaps. This process includes consulting lawyers, CPAs, and other professionals with deep domain knowledge when necessary.

Great entrepreneurs also balance a strong do-it-yourself drive with the understanding that the whole team creates great innovations and succeeds in bringing great products to the world. Along those lines, here's a simple plan for the scrappy early-stage founder who can't afford to hire a startup lawyer or CPA to handle all of the tasks needed to close a funding deal or form the startup:

1. Educate yourself on what's needed. Learn about startup equity structures and issues, legal agreements, financing structures, and other company formation best practices, and then;

2. Get your lawyer involved. Once you thoroughly understand the moving parts and have completed some of the work to the best of your ability, pay your startup-experienced lawyer or other professional to advise you and finalize the legal contracts.

With this self-educating and money-saving sequence in mind, let's dig in to this *Founder's Pocket Guide*.

In This Pocket Guide

The goal of this guide is to help you understand the key moving parts of an investment term sheet, and review typical preferred share rights, preferences, and protections. Along the way, we also provide easy-to-follow examples for the most common calculations related to preferred share equity deals.

Expanding on these fundraising concepts, this *Founder's Pocket Guide* helps startup founders learn:

- **What a term sheet is** and how to summarize the most important deal terms for your fundraising and startup building goals.

- **How preferred stock shares differ from common shares,** with review of how each key preferred share right and preference is tied to the investor's shares.

- **Key terms and definitions** associated with equity fundraising, such as pre-money valuation, founder dilution, and down round.

- **How to decipher legalese** associated with a term sheet deal, such as *pro rata, fully diluted,* and *pari passu.*

- **The full list of the most common term sheet clauses,** their plain English meaning, and their importance to an early-stage investment deal.

- **Simple math** for the key term sheet financial aspects, including calculating fully diluted shares outstanding, investor equity ownership percentages, and the impact of option pools on founder dilution.

- **Example exit scenarios,** showing how term sheet deal points impact how exit proceeds get divided among investors and founders.

Founder Pro Tips

To further help guide you through the ins and outs of investment term sheets and preferred stock rights, you'll find useful tips throughout this guide that provide deeper insights, insider tips, and additional explanations.

Venture Capital Deal Points

Also throughout this guide, you'll find term sheet sections that are primarily used in venture capital (VC) level deals (as opposed to angel investments). These sections are highlighted with the VC stamp icon.

VC level deals usually involve the negotiation of several millions of dollars, and the more capital being raised, the more conditions, preferred share rights, and restrictions are placed on the funding deal. Venture capitalists and their lawyers have developed a handful of term sheet clauses that help protect their investments and give them an out if the startup has difficulty growing and ultimately attracting exit partners or becoming a viable IPO candidate. The VC icon helps to highlight these VC-specific deal points.

Term Sheet Basics

This section reviews several basic concepts related to investment term sheets including the basic purpose of the term sheet in an equity investment deal, understanding preferred stock shares, and reviewing several terms and definitions needed to fully understand how term sheet elements affect your equity funding plans.

What is a Term Sheet?

If angels or venture capitalists are interested in investing in your startup, they will begin discussing the general terms of an investment deal, including how large an investment they might make, what percentages of equity will result for the investors, the startup's pre-money valuation, board structure and seats, and so on. The term sheet is a document that outlines these factors, as well as other protections and rights the investors would like to establish.

Most importantly from the investor's perspective, the term sheet defines the parameters of the preferred stock that represents their ownership in the startup. Preferred shares get additional rights or "preferences" tied to them, adding to the protections the investors get, such as getting paid back first in line in the event of an exit (the sale of the startup to a larger company). The term sheet outlines these preferences and provides a mechanism to negotiate back and forth quickly, without having to modify and send the full blown legal documents such as the stock purchase agreement each time.

Not a Contract

A term sheet is not a contract or a promise to invest, but rather an agreement in principle that outlines the terms of the investment deal. Just because you have a signed term sheet does not mean the investment deal is completed.

Digging deeper, term sheets cover four key categories of the proposed investment deal, including:

Financial Deal Points. These sections of the term sheet simply outline the financial terms of the investment deal, including the investment amount, the pre-money valuation of the startup, the stock price, and other direct financial elements of the deal.

Preferred Share Rights. These sections or clauses define the rights attached to the stock shares the investors will get as a result of the investment. As you will read later in this guide, numerous different preferred share rights affect the financial outcome of the investment deal, such as liquidation preferences, anti-dilution rights, and participation rights.

We're In, Let's Make a Deal

If an investor presents you with a term sheet, it means a lot of other things are right in your startup. The investor believes your team can execute your vision of the business, that the market you are targeting is big enough to support your financial projections, that your target customer will continue to sign up and pay, and so on. A term sheet signals that investors want in, and from there, it's just a matter of hammering out the details.

Investor Control and Protections. In addition to financial advantages attached to preferred shares, many term sheet sections increase the influence the investor has over the startup, including items such as voting rights, the right to limit the founders from taking on additional investments, or selling the company.

Investment Prerequisites. These sections summarize additional conditions that the startup must meet in order to close the investment deal, such as founder employment agreements or invention assignment agreements signed by founders and all employees.

Understanding Share Types

One of the main purposes of term sheet for an equity funding deal is to specify the type of shares the investors get and define special rights assigned to those shares.

In return for an equity stake in a startup, the startup issues either common stock or preferred stock. Prior to any outside investment in the startup, most startups only have common shares—the most basic unit of equity ownership. Founders, friends and family investors, and in some cases employees own these common shares. When outside investors enter the equation, they typically require a new class of stock to be created—preferred shares.

As a startup founder, you need to understand the differences between the two types of shares and how they affect the equity structure in your company. The following sections outline the key differences in the share types.

Preferred Shares

Seasoned investors such as angels and venture capital firms (VCs) usually request preferred shares when they invest in a startup. "Preferred" means that they get certain rights with their shares. These rights provide the preferred shareholder protections, such as getting paid back first before common stock shareholders. As mentioned earlier, one of the primary missions of a term sheet is to define the preferred share rights associated with the investment deal.

Rights included with preferred shares might include:

- Liquidation Preference

- Participation Preference

- Anti-Dilution Preference

- Voting Rights

Later sections explain each of these preferred share rights in detail.

Common Shares

In contrast to investor-owned preferred shares, founders and employees typically hold common shares. When founders form the corporate entity, they decide what percentage of the company each founder owns, and issue enough common shares to each founder to represent their respective percentage ownership.

Common shares have no special rights or leverage. They are the most basic representation of ownership in the company. The number of common shares you own represents your percentage ownership in the company.

Common shares typically afford you voting rights on key decisions in the startup, although startups can create non-voting common shares. Your percentage ownership determines the weight of your vote. If you own 55% of the common shares, your vote has a weight of 55% relative to the other voters.

Due to preferred share rights such as the liquidation preference, common share owners are typically last in line to get paid in the event of an exit or dissolution of the company. Debt holders such as banks or other lenders get paid first, followed by any preferred shareholders, and then common stock holders.

Specific Term Sheet Terminology

A few terms show up over and over again in terms sheet clauses as well as in investor discussions—*fully diluted* and *pro rata*. Understanding what these terms mean is critical to calculating the impact of a funding deal on your founder's equity and understanding the investor's rights to acquire more stock in any future funding deals. Let's review these terms.

Fully Diluted

In order to determine any individual shareholder's true ownership percentage of the startup, you need to know how big the whole startup is in terms of stock shares. The term *fully diluted* refers to this process of sizing up the total number of shares that have been issued or promised to the various stakeholders of the startup.

Sizing up the total ownership pie means you must take into account all stock issued to the founders and investors, as well as all stock options and warrants that were not yet actually issued but rather promised or granted to employees, investors, or other stakeholders.

Include Stock Options. Stock options are typically used as a form of non-cash compensation for employees and other stakeholders. The stock option gives the option holder the right to buy the startup's stock at a low price, and therefore own a portion of the startup for very little cash outlay. To facilitate the stock option process, the startup designates a certain percentage of the startup's equity to be used for the option incentive plan—this percentage of equity is called the option pool. Stock options assigned to the option pool are included in the fully diluted basis total.

Include Warrants. Other securities types such as warrants are also included in the fully diluted calculation. Similar to stock options, warrants give their holder the option to buy the company stock as a certain price over a certain time frame. Even though an investor may choose not to exercise warrants or exercise conditions (such as exercise-by dates) may become irrelevant if the company dissolves first, the warrants still must be counted in the fully diluted basis. Warrants make the overall share pie bigger and dilute the founder's ownership.

The following steps outline the process for calculating the number of fully diluted shares outstanding:

1. Account for all common shares issued to founders and other stakeholders.

2. Convert all preferred shares to common shares. Usually preferred shares convert on a one-to-one (1:1) basis, but anti-dilution provisions could change this to say two-to-one (2:1) or other ratios as dictated by the anti-dilution provisions outlined in the term sheet.

3. Convert all issued stock options to their common share equivalent.

4. Account for all stock options reserved for future grant.

5. Convert all warrants to their common share basis.

6. Add everything up. The total you arrive at will be the "fully diluted basis."

Next, to calculate an individual shareholder's equity ownership percentage, divide the number of shares held by the shareholder by the fully diluted number.

Now review a simplified example. Let's say you've calculated that there are 10 million fully diluted shares outstanding for your startup. As an major investor (Investor A in the graphic below), you own two million shares. If you divided your shares by the fully diluted shares as illustrated in the formula below, the result is .2 or 20% ownership in the startup.

INVESTOR A
SHARES
2 MILLION
———————
10 MILLION
FULLY DILUTED
SHARES
OUTSTANDING

=

INVESTOR A
OWNERSHIP
20%
ON A FULLY
DILUTED BASIS

Pro Rata

Several clauses in a term sheet will refer to an investor's *pro rata* share. For example, "Investors are required to purchase their pro rata share of the securities."

Pro rata is Latin for *by calculation* and means proportional ownership. Think of pro rata as legal shorthand for saying "your proportional share of." Example phrases in term sheets include:

> "The investor's pro rata share of the Series A Preferred stock."

> "Your pro rata share of fully diluted shares outstanding."

For example, a term sheet clause may stipulate that the investor has the right to buy a fully diluted pro rata share of any new round of stock the startup might issue later. Therefore, if the investor currently owns 25% of the company (on a fully diluted basis), he has the right to purchase up to 25% of the new stock offering.

Startup Funding Terminology

To lay the groundwork for an in-depth term sheet review, let's start by reviewing several additional key terms you are likely to encounter when working any startup fundraising effort:

- **Equity.** The ownership of the startup—who owns how much. In the most common sequence, the founders own 100% equity of the startup at formation, then give up chunks of ownership (stock shares) to outside investors in exchange for cash investments. Portions of equity are also given to key employees in the form of stock options as additional compensation for their contributions to the startup's efforts. If the startup gets acquired by a larger company (an event called an exit), percentage equity ownership determines how much each stock owner gets paid.

- **Pre-Money Valuation.** The value placed on a startup before an investment round. The pre-money valuation is a key point of negotiation between founders and equity investors.

- **Post-Money Valuation.** The value of the startup after the investment round. The investment amount + the pre-money valuation = the post-money valuation.

- **Founder Dilution.** The amount of ownership given up by startup founders in exchange for cash injected by an investor. Dilution is expressed as a percentage— "the founders are willing to accept a 20% dilution in exchange for a $200,000 angel fund investment."

- **Investor Dilution.** Founders are not the only stakeholders that give up equity as new investors come into the funding picture. Existing investors can also be required to withstand a reduction in their ownership percentage in the startup. If the startup raises multiple rounds of equity investment, early investors will give up some ownership to new investors. Anti-dilution rights attached to preferred shares are one way investors attempt to limit their exposure to dilution.

- **Priced Round.** When the startup closes an equity investment deal with investors, the valuation of the company is established and the price per share of company stock is calculated. Prior to a startup's first equity fundraising deal, the price per share of stock is set very low (typically $0.0001 per share), or otherwise unpriced. In the convertible debt context, the next priced round typically triggers the note to convert to equity.

- **Down Round.** When founders accept an equity investment at a valuation lower than the previously established valuation. The company is worth less now than it was at the previous investment round.

- **Raise or Round (Investment Round).** The process and result of raising money for your startup is called a round or a raise. Whether you are at the beginning stages of the money raising process, or have just put an investor's money in the bank, each round is given a name or designation, such as seed round or Series A round.

- **Seed Round.** In common usage, a seed round can be any investment in a startup used to start the company and create its first products or services. The seed round can include money coming from the founders themselves, friends and family, or other supporters associated with the entrepreneurs. In contrast, the high tech Silicon Valley definition of seed round is a bit different. Many large VCs have established seed funds with the purpose of backing very early innovations (almost to the point of experiments) that can disrupt very large industries. The amounts invested in seed rounds by these VCs are sometimes large ($1, $2, or even $3 million), as compared to angel funding rounds in the sub-$1 million range.

- **Series A, Series B, and so on.** Series A is a term used to mean many things, but typically, a Series A is the first Venture Capital level investment round. Additional investments from institutional investors follow the same pattern, Series B, Series C, and so on. Also note that VCs are in the business of investing other institutions' money, not personal money from angels or friends and family investors.

- **VC.** Short for venture capital, VCs are large investment funds seeking out high growth startups that have proven new technology and new markets. Venture capitalists are investing other people's money, from sources such as private foundations, pension plans, university capital funds, and so on. This is one of the major differences between angels and VCs. As a result, VCs often can and will exert much more control over a startup, such as installing an experienced CEO and requiring a board of directors (BOD) seat. That being said, because VCs have access to much larger pools of money, the scale and terms of a VC deal can differ greatly from an angel deal.

- **Angel Investors.** Angels or angel investors are high net worth individuals that invest their own money in startups and early stage ventures, either independently, or in organized angel groups (also called angel investor groups). Angels invest in segments and industries that are experiencing high growth and tend to invest in startups that are at the earliest stage of the company, hoping to realize large returns on their investment. Investing at such an early stage is very risky, so seasoned angel investors tend to make lots of small investments in startups, building a portfolio of 20 or more companies. If one or two startups hit it big, the angels get the returns they are looking for.

Deconstructing a Term Sheet

The sections that follow deconstruct a term sheet into its elemental parts, explaining what each section means and how it relates of other sections of the term sheet. You'll see plain English explanations of legal language where needed and numerous graphic examples that help show the meaning and impact of a term sheet or preferred share clause.

To help organize the deconstruction effort, I've divided typical term sheet parts into two main groups—financial term sheet parameters, and investor control and protection term sheet parameters. Let's get started with the first group, the financial parameters.

Financial Term Sheet Parameters

This group of term sheet parameters or sections enables both investors and founders to calculate the impact of the investment being considered.

This group includes key deal parameters such as the security type, pre-money valuation, the investment amount, share price, and number of shares being purchased by the investor. Outlining the financial components enables calculation of the investor's ownership percentage of the company.

Additional term sheet sections such as stock option pools, dividends, and liquidation preferences related to the financial aspect of the investment deal are also included in this group.

Type of Security

This section is listed at the beginning of the term sheet and defines what the type or class of shares will be called.

Because almost the entire point of a term sheet is to define the rights and preferences attached to the preferred shares the investor is buying, this section of the term sheet must name or define what the preferred stock class is called.

Example security names include:

- Convertible Preferred Stock

- Series A Convertible Preferred Stock

- Series Seed Preferred Stock

 Convertible to What?

As founders gain experience with equity fundraising, they are likely to hear a deal structure referred to as "Convertible Preferred." The preferred shares purchased by the investor will ultimately convert into common shares of the startup—this is the convertible context. Don't confuse this type of conversion with that of convertible debt deals. In convertible debt funding, the investment starts out as a loan to the startup (with interest and other debt conditions), and later converts to equity (stock) in the company.

Investment Amount

This section lists the total dollar amount of the proposed investment. If the startup initiates the term sheet (as opposed to an investor-initiated term sheet), this section may outline the parameters of the total raise amount being sought by the startup, as well as any limitations or thresholds being established around the funding raise process. The second example below illustrates this intent.

Example Wordings

Amount of Financing: $500,000

Amount of Financing: Intended offering is $500,000. The minimum subscription amount before first closing is $125,000.

(In this example wording, the subscription amount language means investors must commit at least a total amount of $125,000 before the startup can close a partial deal and put the money in the bank.)

Pre-Money Valuation

This section of the term sheet details the pre-money valuation the investors and founders have agreed upon.

When founders sell equity in their startup to an outside

investor such as an angel group or venture capital firm, the investor trades cash for a percentage ownership of the startup corporation.

To determine how much of the startup (the percentage) the investor's cash buys him/her, the total value (or valuation) of the startup needs to be agreed on before the investment occurs. So you can think of the pre-money valuation as the "valuation before investment."

This equation with example valuation and investment amounts shows how pre-money and post-money fit together.

Next, the percentage ownership purchased by the investor is expressed by this equation, using the same example investment and post-money valuation amounts:

The pre-money valuation can also appear in the "Price Per Share" section (described shortly), because the price per share is calculated by dividing the pre-money valuation by the total number of shares owned by the current stakeholders of the company.

Many term sheets skip the pre-money valuation section and reference the capitalization table of the company, usually attached as an Exhibit to the term sheet. The capitalization table (cap table) will include the pre-money valuation, ownership percentages, share price, and number of shares owned by each stakeholder.

Example Wording

> **Valuation:** $2,000,000 pre-money valuation, fully diluted, the total number of shares to include an unallocated employee pool of at least 20% of the total, in addition to the founder's shares.

 Option Pool and Valuation Coupling.

Savvy founders know that seasoned investors like VCs often require the startup to create a stock option plan as part of the investment deal, and the investors want the option pool to be included as part of the pre-money valuation. For example, the startup might carve out an option pool of 20% of the equity of the company to give key employees and stakeholders, and that carve out is taken from the founders' equity. In other words, the founders take the dilution hit of the option pool creation. For this reason, founders should make sure they understand whether the option pool creation is pre-money or post-money.

Price Per Share

This section of the term sheet lists the price per share the investors will pay for the stock of the startup company.

The price per share is calculated by dividing the agreed on pre-money valuation by the total number of shares outstanding in the startup (before the investors come into play). This equation shows the calculation:

The share price calculation is where the term *number of fully diluted shares outstanding* typically comes into play. Fully diluted is investor/lawyer speak meaning the options pool and other forms of stock (such as warrants) must be included in the share total as described earlier. And, since this calculation we are dividing the pre-money valuation by that share total, it means the founders are taking the dilution hit of the option pool.

Example Wording

> **Price Per Share:** $0.21.00 per share (the "Original Purchase Price"). The Original Purchase Price represents a fully-diluted pre-money valuation of [$2,000,000] two million. The Company's current capitalization is set forth in the capitalization table attached as Exhibit A."

Number of Shares

ALTERNATE SECTION WORDING: SHARES | SHARES PURCHASED |TOTAL SECURITIES OFFERED

This section of the term sheet lists the number of shares that will be purchased by the investor.

The number of shares purchased by the investor is calculated by dividing the investment amount by the price per share of the company's stock. This example shows a number of shares calculation:

$$\frac{\text{INVESTMENT AMOUNT } \$1 \text{ MILLION}}{\$0.20 \text{ PRICE PER SHARE}} = \text{INVESTOR SHARES } 5 \text{ MILLION}$$

This section may also reference the cap table of the startup as an attachment or exhibit tacked onto the end of the term sheet.

Example Wording

Number of Shares: Five Million (5,000,000) Series A Preferred Stock

Conversion

ALTERNATE SECTION WORDING: CONVERSION RIGHT | AUTOMATIC CONVERSION | OPTIONAL CONVERSION

In plain English, the conversion clause says that the investor will receive the preferred shares with special rights, and these shares can be converted to common shares at any time.

When it comes to calculating the exact ownership percentages of the company, the calculations are all performed based on the total number of fully diluted shares outstanding. As related earlier, to get to a fully diluted status, all share types need to be converted to their common share equivalent—the most basic form of ownership in the startup.

The conversion clause also typically includes the standard conversion ratio of one-to-one (1:1)—one share of preferred stock converts to one share of common stock. As you will read in the anti-dilution section, the anti-dilution calculations take advantage of the conversion process and modify the conversion ratio in favor of the preferred share investor, giving him or her more shares of common stock for each share of preferred stock, and therefore avoiding or reducing the dilution of the Preferred Share investors stock relative to founders who typically don't have anti-dilution rights.

 New Shares Created For Conversion.

As part of finalizing the investment deal involving preferred shares, the startup's Articles of Incorporation are amended to create the new class of stock (the preferred shares), and the matching number of common shares is also authorized to accommodate the preferred-to-common conversion process, whenever it may later occur. Conversion to common does not take away shares from any existing common shareholders—founders, employees, or others.

Conversion clauses can be as simple as just stating that the preferred shares can convert to common shares at any time. Some term sheets go further to define circumstances in which the preferred shares automatically convert to common shares. Either way, the basic principle of converting to common shares is covered by the conversion clause.

Example Wordings

> **Optional Conversion:** Each share of Series A Convertible Preferred Stock is convertible at any time to one share of Common Stock.

Automatic Conversion: Each share of Series A Convertible Preferred Stock shall automatically convert into one share of Common Stock upon (i) simultaneously with the first closing of public offering; or (ii) consent of the holders of a majority of the Series A Convertible Preferred Shares then outstanding.

Dividends

Dividends are one way for investors to realize an upside on an investment. Similar to an interest rate on a loan, dividends are expressed as a percentage of the investment amount. Keep in mind that investors primarily hope to get paid back when the startup becomes very successful and gets acquired by a larger entity. Periodic dividends just sweeten the pot.

In basic terms, a dividend is a distribution of the startup's profits to its shareholders, usually paid in cash or stock. The startup's board of directors (BOD) decides if the company is in position to pay dividends and usually addresses the decision to pay dividends one time each fiscal year.

Early-Stage Startup Reality

Early-stage startups are usually not in the financial position to pay out cash dividends to investors. Growing the startup usually requires reinvesting any extra cash back into the business, and therefore the BOD will not vote to pay out dividends. However, if the startup is successful and gets acquired, any unpaid dividends owed investors will be included in the exit proceeds payout to the investors. So dividends provide an additional benefit to investors in the event of an exit.

There are two types of dividends—cumulative and non-cumulative. Here's a look at the differences between the two.

Cumulative Dividends

With a cumulative dividend, the dividend amount owed to the preferred share investor is calculated annually. If the BOD votes to pay dividends for the current fiscal year, the startup pays the dividend amount owed to the investor. If the BOD elects not to pay the dividend, the amount owed to the preferred share investor is carried over to the next fiscal year.

For example, say the startup agrees to pay a 10% dividend on an investment of $5,000,000, equaling a dividend of $500,000 for the current fiscal year. If the BOD votes to pay dividends, then the preferred share investor gets the $500,000. If the startup is not in position to pay the dividend and so the BOD votes accordingly, the $500,000 owed is carried forward to the next year. Each year's dividend owed rolls over or accumulates until the startup can pay the dividends owed. In this example, after three years, cumulative dividends owed the investor would total $1,500,000 (three x $500,000 annual amount).

Example Wording

> **Dividends:** Dividends on the Series A Convertible Preferred Shares carry an annual 8% cumulative dividend [compounded annually], payable solely upon a liquidation event.

Why Cumulative Dividends Are Doubly Bad.

Many times the term sheet includes a clause that states that cumulative dividends will by paid upon a liquidation event, such as the acquisition of the startup. In this case, it is possible that a large dollar amount of dividends owed has accumulated. So, the founders must use part of their exit payout to pay the dividends owed, reducing the founders' proceeds. For this reason, most founders try to avoid agreeing to cumulative dividends.

Non-Cumulative Dividends

With non-cumulative dividends, if the BOD decides not to pay dividends in the current fiscal year, then that year's dividends do not carry forward to the next year. So using the example figure used previously, the investor might receive no dividends the first and second years, and $500,000 for the third year, for a total of only $500,000 (versus $1,500,000 owed for the three years if the dividend were cumulative). For this reason, non-cumulative dividends are the most founder-favorable option to negotiate.

Example Wordings

Dividends: Dividends on the Series A Convertible Preferred Shares are neither mandatory nor cumulative. No dividends will be paid on Common stock unless dividends are paid on Series A Convertible Preferred shares.

Dividends: The holders of the Preferred Stock shall be entitled to receive dividends at a rate of X% per share, payable prior and in preference to any declaration or payment of any other dividends, when, and if declared by the Board of Directors. Dividends are neither mandatory nor cumulative.

Liquidation Preference

Liquidation preference refers to what happens if your startup gets acquired, merges with another company, or has to close down. A liquidation preference places the preferred shareholder at the front of the line when it comes to dividing up the proceeds from an exit event. In other words, pay the investors first, then everybody else. It should be noted that the liquidation preference does not affect the equity percentage ownership of the investor, but rather provides a bonus over and above any basic equity-based division of exit proceeds—the examples below should illustrate this idea.

Next to the pre-money valuation of the startup, the liquidation preference is the most negotiated term sheet provision, and there are three main flavors to understand:

- **Non-participating preferred**

- **Participating preferred**

- **Participating preferred with a cap**

To best understand how the liquidation preference comes into play, consider a startup that has just been has been acquired. At this point, the proceeds were divided up among the startup's shareholders—equity investors, founders, management, key employees. So how does a liquidation preference influence how much the investors get? Let's take a look at the three typical options:

35

Non-Participating Preferred

With this type of liquidation preference, the preferred shareholders are first in line to receive their total investment amount (plus any accumulated unpaid dividends) out of the exit proceeds. The investors receive preference over the common shareholders, but they do not get to participate with the common shareholders in splitting up any proceeds left over after the preferred investors get their payout. It's important to note that investors are not really interested in just getting their investment paid back (plus dividends). They are in the deal to win big, so the non-participating preferred liquidation preference is really just an insurance policy, putting the investors first in line in case of an low-value exit or company shut down.

 Liquidation Multiples—1X, 2X, etc.

Some investors also push for a liquidation preference *multiple* to be stated in the liquidation preference section of the term sheet. This means that the preferred shareholder not only gets his or her entire investment out of the sale proceeds (and perhaps participate with the common shareholders), but they also get two times (2X) or even three times (3X) the invested amount, prior to the common shareholders receiving any of the sale proceeds. 2X and 3X multiples are often seen as heavy-handed investor requirements, and founders with any amount of leverage in the investment negotiation should push toward a simple 1X preference.

Participating Preferred

With a participating preferred right attached to the preferred shares, the investor get two benefits over common shareholders when the startup exits:

1. The Preferred Right. As above, the investor has the right to get the entire investment amount (or multiple, as in 2X, or 3X if so defined) paid out of the proceeds from the exit event.

In our example figure below, here's how this shakes out:

A. The startup is being sold for and exit value of $10 million.

B. The investors invested $5 million for 50% of the company, and they have a 1X liquidation preference with participation, therefore they get $5 million of the exit proceeds, first, then;

2. Participation with the Common Shareholders. With this second step, the investor's preferred shares convert to common shares, and the investor gets a portion of the proceeds based on his or her overall pro rata percentage ownership. In our graphic example below:

C. Because the investors also have Participation right, they get to participate with the common shareholders in dividing whatever is left over—in this case they get their pro rata 50% of the remaining $5 million, or $2.5 million.

D. The common shareholders (the founders and employees) get to divide the final $2.5 million of the exit proceeds.

This graphic shows the participating preferred liquidation preference in action.

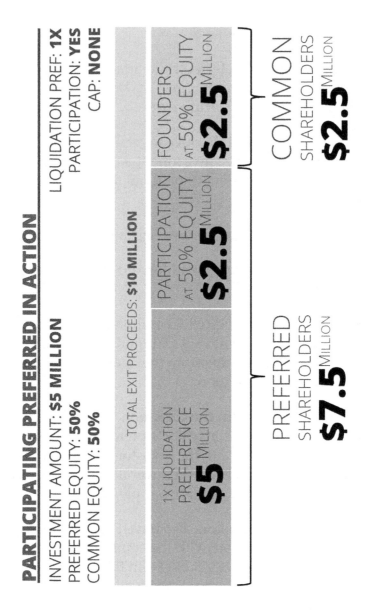

PARTICIPATING PREFERRED IN ACTION

INVESTMENT AMOUNT: **$5 MILLION**
PREFERRED EQUITY: **50%**
COMMON EQUITY: **50%**

LIQUIDATION PREF: **1X**
PARTICIPATION: **YES**
CAP: **NONE**

TOTAL EXIT PROCEEDS: **$10 MILLION**

1X LIQUIDATION PREFERENCE
$5 MILLION

PARTICIPATION AT 50% EQUITY
$2.5 MILLION

FOUNDERS AT 50% EQUITY
$2.5 MILLION

PREFERRED SHAREHOLDERS
$7.5 MILLION

COMMON SHAREHOLDERS
$2.5 MILLION

As you can see in the graphic example, a liquidation preference with participation can be very favorable for investors, and can result in founders getting a much smaller percentage of the exit value. Placing a cap on the liquidation preference is a good middle ground for founders to pursue, as explained next.

Participating Preferred with a Cap

A middle ground between non-participating and participating preferred, this option limits or places a cap on the total amount of exit proceeds the investor can receive under the liquidation preference.

In our example, the startup is being sold for $10 million, investors own 50% of the company, and they have a 1X liquidation preference with a $6 million cap. As you can see in the graphic below, the investors get their $5 million investment back, plus they participate in dividing the rest of the exit proceeds with the common shareholders, but only up to the cap amount. This gives the investors a total of $6 million from the sale of the company.

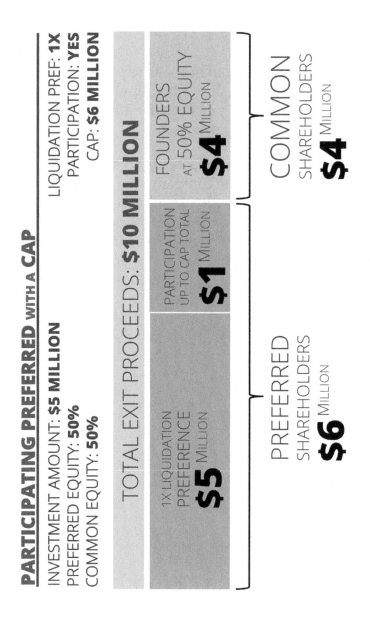

PARTICIPATING PREFERRED WITH A CAP

INVESTMENT AMOUNT: **$5 MILLION**
PREFERRED EQUITY: **50%**
COMMON EQUITY: **50%**

LIQUIDATION PREF: **1X**
PARTICIPATION: **YES**
CAP: **$6 MILLION**

TOTAL EXIT PROCEEDS: **$10 MILLION**

1X LIQUIDATION PREFERENCE
$5 MILLION

PARTICIPATION UP TO CAP TOTAL
$1 MILLION

FOUNDERS AT 50% EQUITY
$4 MILLION

PREFERRED SHAREHOLDERS
$6 MILLION

COMMON SHAREHOLDERS
$4 MILLION

As you can see in this example, the liquidation preference gives the investors more than 50% of the exit proceeds, even though they own just 50% of the total company.

Converting to Common to Get the Highest Return

Note again that the preferred shareholders always have the option to convert their shares to common shares, ignoring all of the liquidation preference calculations all together, and sidestepping the cap. In our previous example above, the investors don't benefit by just converting to their 50% common basis, because their participating preferred with a cap give them $6 million, or $1 million more than their 50% common basis would yield.

But, in the case of a high exit value ($50 million in the graphic example below) the investors are better off ignoring the liquidation preference entirely and converting to common shares. Remember, the investor's original cash injection gave them a 50% ownership in the startup. Therefore, converting to common shares gives the investor a 50% stake in the $50,000,000 exit proceeds, or $25,000,000, far exceeding the capped $6,000,000 liquidation preference in the prior graphic.

CONVERTING TO COMMON SHARES

INVESTMENT AMOUNT: **$5 MILLION**
PREFERRED EQUITY: **50%**
COMMON EQUITY: **50%**

LIQUIDATION PREF: **1X**
PARTICIPATION: **YES**
CAP: **$6 MILLION**

**DUE TO THE CAP ($6 MILLION), INVESTORS
WILL IGNORE THE LIQUIDATION PREFERENCE**

AND CONVERT TO COMMON TO GET 50% OF THE $50 MILLION EXIT

TOTAL EXIT PROCEEDS: **$50 MILLION**

INVESTORS
AT 50% EQUITY
$25 MILLION

FOUNDERS
AT 50% EQUITY
$25 MILLION

Example Wording

> **Liquidation Preference:** In the event of a sale of all or substantially all of the assets, merger, consolidation, liquidation, dissolution or winding up of the Company (a "Liquidation Event"), the holders of the Series A Convertible Preferred Shares shall be entitled to receive an amount (the "Liquidation Amount") equal to the original purchase price, plus all declared and unpaid dividends.

Option Pools

ALTERNATE SECTION WORDING: OPTIONS | OPTION INCENTIVE PLAN

 It is common for institutional investors such as VCs to require the startup to establish a stock incentive plan in the form of stock options. The options are used to attract and retain key employees and sometimes as a noncash payment mechanism for service providers such as developers, accountants, and lawyers.

The option pool is expressed as a percentage of the overall company equity (in common stock shares). The option pool shares are set aside and later granted to employees and other stakeholders over time.

The option pool must be carved out of the overall equity of the startup, and therefore is included in the company capitalization table.

The option pool section of the term sheet outlines the investor's requirement for the option pool creation, as well as size of the pool. Pool sizes of 10% to 20% are common.

Who Takes the Dilution Hit?

The key equation a founder must consider is whose equity does the option pool come from—only the founder's equity, or both the founder's and the investor's. Of course, most investors hope to push the founder(s) to create the option pool out of the founder's equity before the investor's cash is injected (pre-money), resulting in the founder(s) getting diluted by the option pool percentage. Or, will the investor allow the option pool to be carved out of the equity ownership after his or her cash is invested (post money), resulting in both the founder(s) and the new investor sharing in the dilution effect of the option pool. The common practice is for the option pool to be established on the pre-money valuation, and therefore the founders and any other existing shareholders are hit with the dilution effect of the option pool, but this can certainly be negotiated.

Example Wording

Option Pool: Prior to the Closing, the Company will reserve 20% of its Common Stock shares, on a fully diluted basis, to be available for future issuances to directors, officers, employees, and consultants.

Anti-Dilution

 This clause protects the preferred shareholders by preserving existing ownership percentages in a later investment round, especially a down round where the new investor wants a lower valuation for the startup. Say your startup is facing a down round, your current investors don't want to dilute their ownership percentage of the company—that is, if an investor owns 25% of the company now, the investor must still own 25% after the down round.

Let's take a look at the sort of circumstances that might trigger a down round to illustrate the need to address anti-dilution in the term sheet. Say a startup is doing OK, but not great. So far, the company has not been hitting key milestones such as revenue growth. The startup is now in discussions with new investors to raise more money to fund new needs and allow more time to get on track.

As a result of missing the milestones, the founders can't convince potential new investors that the startup's valuation should be higher for this next round. For example, the new investors will only agree to a pre-money valuation of $4 million, or $1 million lower than the previous investment round. That lower valuation would therefore make the new round a down round.

If the founders and current investors go through with accepting the new funding (which they almost have to), when the new investors come into the picture, the existing investors (including founders and other shareholders) will own a smaller percentage of the company; they get diluted.

The anti-dilution section of the term sheet is designed to either prevent or reduce the dilutive effects of a down round for the current preferred stock investors. Unfortunately, the founders and other common shareholders do not benefit from anti-dilution, but rather bear the brunt of the dilution, as you will see below.

Pro Tip

Conversion Price Adjustment

Note that the anti-dilution language does not cause new stock shares to be issued to the preferred shareholders during a down round, but rather, it dictates the conversion formula used when the preferred shares are converted to common shares, as triggered by a liquidity event such as the acquisition of the startup. Under normal circumstances, the term sheet defines that preferred shares convert to common share on a 1:1 basis. One share preferred converts to one share of common. The anti-dilution formulas change this conversion ratio at the time of conversion, usually the sale of the startup.

Anti-dilution clauses can take three typical forms—none at all, full ratchet, or weighted average—explained next.

No Anti-Dilution Protection

With no anti-dilution protection stated in the term sheet, the investors will share in whatever dilution takes place in the event of a down round.

This graphic shows the resulting ownership percentages after another example down round, with no anti-dilution protection for the preferred share investors—the Series A (Round 1) investors go from a 40% equity stake down to a

20% stake. The 50% reduction in equity reflects the new pre-money valuation for Round 2 ($500,000), which is half the post-money valuation for Round 1 ($1,000,000). Note also the founders take a 50% dilution hit in order to raise the new money from the Series B (Round 2) investors.

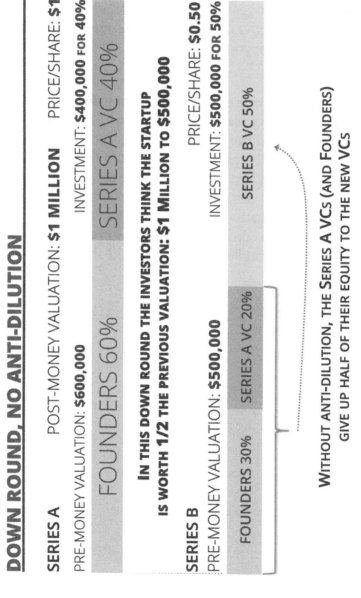

Full Ratchet Anti-Dilution

With full ratchet anti-dilution, in the event of a down round, the current preferred share investor's share price is adjusted all the way down to the level needed so that two things happen:

1. The new investor gets their percentage. The new investor gets the percentage ownership negotiated in the new down round investment, 50% in our example graphics.

2. The current preferred share investor with full ratchet anti-dilution protection maintains his/her ownership percentage in the startup, 40% in our example below. To maintain the preferred shareholder's ownership percentage, when the preferred shares convert to common (say during an exit event), the conversion calculations include the anti-dilution adjustment, resulting in a conversion to common shares at a lower share price that keeps the preferred shares investor's 40% intact.

DOWN ROUND, FULL RATCHET ANTI-DILUTION

SERIES A

PRE-MONEY VALUATION: **$600,000**

POST-MONEY VALUATION: **$1 MILLION**

INVESTMENT: **$400,000 FOR 40%**

FOUNDERS 60%

SERIES A VC 40%

IN THIS DOWN ROUND THE INVESTORS THINK THE STARTUP IS WORTH 1/2 THE PREVIOUS VALUATION: $1 MILLION TO $500,000

SERIES B

PRE-MONEY VALUATION: **$500,000**

POST-MONEY VALUATION: **$1 MILLION**

INVESTMENT: **$500,000 FOR 50%**

FOUNDERS 10%

SERIES A VC 40%

SERIES B VC 50%

THE **FULL RATCHET** ANTI-DILUTION PRESERVES THE SERIES A VCs EQUITY AT THE EXPENSE OF THE FOUNDERS

A full-ratchet scenario dilutes founder ownership dramatically, so this anti-dilution method is unfavorable to founders. The effect of this is that the preferred share investors get more shares for their investment, and therefore own a greater percentage of the startup, at the expense of the founders and other common shareholders. Keep in mind, when founders get diluted, they are not actually giving up any shares they hold, but rather, new shares are being issued to outside investors (Series B VC in our example), therefore the total number of shares has increased, reducing the overall percentage the founders hold of the company.

Weighted Average Anti-Dilution

The weighted average anti-dilution calculation provides a more balanced form of reducing the impact of a down round on investors and founders. Using the weighted average formula (below) results in:

1. Founders get diluted (but not as much as in a full ratchet scenario).

2. Preferred share investors get diluted a little bit, as opposed to not at all in a full ratchet scenario.

The weighted average formula takes into account the total shares outstanding in relation to the number of shares owned by the preferred share investor (the one with anti-dilution protection.) The more shares (percentage ownership) the preferred share investor holds, the more the weighted average formula works to reduce the dilution impact on the investment.

This graphic shows how the weighted average approach balances the dilution impact between preferred share investors and the founders.

DOWN ROUND, WEIGHTED AVERAGE ANTI-DILUTION

SERIES A

PRE-MONEY VALUATION: **$600,000**   POST-MONEY VALUATION: **$1 MILLION**

INVESTMENT: **$400,000** FOR **40%**

FOUNDERS 60%

SERIES A VC 40%

**IN THIS DOWN ROUND THE INVESTORS THINK THE STARTUP
IS WORTH 1/2 THE PREVEIOUS VALUATION: $1 MILLON TO $500,000**

SERIES B

PRE-MONEY VALUATION: **$500,000**   POST-MONEY VALUATION: **$1 MILLION**

INVESTMENT: **$500,000** FOR **50%**

FOUNDERS 24%   SERIES A VC 26%

SERIES B VC 50%

THE WEIGHTED AVERAGE ANTI-DILUTION BALANCES THE
DILUTION BETWEEN THE SERIES A VCs EQUITY AND THE FOUNDERS

The weighted average method is favorable to founders.
If you must accept some form of anti-dilution in your term sheet negotiations, weighted average is the one to go for. As stated earlier, full ratchet anti-dilution is very unfavorable to founders.

Example Wording

Anti-Dilution Provisions: In the event that the Company issues additional securities at a purchase price less than the current Series A Preferred conversion price, such conversion price shall be adjusted in accordance with the following formula:

Alternative 1: "Typical" weighted average:

$$CP2 = CP1 * (A+B) / (A+C)$$

CP2 = Series A Conversion Price in effect immediately after new issue

CP1 = Series A Conversion Price in effect immediately prior to new issue

A = Number of shares of Common Stock deemed to be outstanding immediately prior to new issue (includes all shares of outstanding common stock, all shares of outstanding preferred stock on an as-converted basis, and all outstanding options on an as-exercised basis; and does not include any convertible securities converting into this round of financing)

B = Aggregate consideration received by the Corporation with respect to the new issue divided by CP1

C = Number of shares of stock issued in the subject transaction

Alternative 2: Full Ratchet: The conversion price will be reduced to the price at which the new shares are issued.

Pay to Play

 A pay to play clause is intended to create an incentive for existing preferred share investors to invest on a pro rata basis in future financing rounds. It spells out that if the existing investors choose not to participate in future rounds, they will lose some or all of their preferential rights.

Here's how it works. If the preferred share investor participates in investing more in the down round, then his or her anti-dilution rights (as defined in the preferred share term sheet) remain in effect. If the preferred share investor chooses not to continue to help fund the startup during a down round, the investor loses any anti-dilution rights, and perhaps other or all preferred share rights. In other words, if you fail to pay, you don't get to play (with your preferred share rights intact).Pay to play is primarily used to incent investors to keep funding the startup during a down round with two typical disincentives for not participating:

1. Take away some preferred rights. Implementing this option creates a new class of preferred shares that do not include the anti-dilution rights (often referred to as *shadow preferred*), and automatically converts the non-participating investors preferred shares into the new shadow preferred shares.

2. Take away all preferred share rights and protections. An extreme version of the pay to play clause is to force the conversion of the investors preferred shares into common shares, thus stripping away all of the preferred share rights and protections.

Pay to play is almost exclusively a VC level provision. Term sheets for angel level investments typically do not include a pay to play clause. Angels and angel groups do not have the levels of capital needed to participate in VC level deals, so a provision that forces them to continue to invest does not make sense. On the other hand, it can makes sense to incent Series A VCs to stay with the company through a Series B or C round, and this is where the pay to play element most often occurs.

Example Wordings

Pay to Play: [Unless the holders of [__]% of the Series A elect otherwise,] on any subsequent [down] round all [Major] Investors are required to purchase their pro rata share of the securities set aside by the Board for purchase by the [Major] Investors. All shares of Series A Preferred of any [Major] Investor failing to do so will automatically [lose anti-dilution rights] [lose liquidation preferences] [lose the right to participate in future rounds] [convert to Common Stock and lose the right to a Board seat, if applicable]

Pay to Play: In the event that any holder of shares of Series A Preferred Stock does not participate in a Qualified Financing by purchasing in the aggregate, in such Qualified Financing and within the time period specified by the Corporation such holder's Pro Rata Amount, [then each share] of Series A Preferred Stock held by such holder shall automatically, and without any further action on the part of such holder, be converted into shares of Common Stock at the Series A Conversion Price in effect immediately prior to the consummation of such Qualified Financing, effective upon, subject to, and concurrently with, the consummation of the Qualified Financing.

Warrants

Warrants are a type of security that gives investors the option to buy more stock over a designated timeframe (three to seven years is a common range) and at a specific price.

Warrants are an add-on to an investment deal, sweetening the deal by enabling the investor to buy more shares in the startup. Founders often use warrants to entice investors to come aboard at the early and risky stage of the company.

If the startup does really well, warrant holders can buy more stock (called *exercising the warrants*), thus increasing the holder's stake in the company. If the startup does poorly and fails to increase its value, the warrant holder likely will not exercise the warrants.

Three parameters define the details of a typical warrant clause—the term, the coverage, and the price:

Term. The term of the warrants identifies the window of time that the investor has the option to exercise the warrants. Investors like long term durations, giving them and the startup the most amount of time to become successful. All involved hope to have a liquidity event, at which time the warrants typically automatically exercise in favor of the preferred share investor.

Coverage. Warrant coverage spells out the number of shares (or the dollar amount) the investor is entitled to buy. The clause language typically expresses the coverage amount as a percentage of the overall investment amount, say 20% (.20) coverage of a $500,000 investment. That example works out as $100,000 (.20 X $500,000) worth of shares the investor can purchase at the share price listed in the clause.

Price. The price paid (referred to as the *exercise price* of the warrant) is specified in the term sheet clause. This price is typically the same share price as the current investment round, or the share price of a future funding round.

Example Wording

> **Warrants:** The Preferred Share investors shall receive ___ year warrants in the amount of ___ Warrants for each share of Preferred Stock purchased in this round of financing. The Warrants shall be exercisable for [Common Stock][Preferred Stock] at $___ per share. The Warrants shall contain a cashless exercise feature and customary representations, warranties, and other terms.

Legal Fees

ALTERNATE SECTION WORDING: FINANCING EXPENSES | COMPANY OBLIGATIONS | EXPENSES

This section of the term sheet states which party pays the legal fees associated with the investment deal. It's common or the startup to pay the legal fees, but startup founders can use some of the proceeds of the investment to do so. However, in some cases, the startup splits the legal fees with the investor.

Example Wording

> **Legal Fees:** The Company will bear all legal and other expenses with respect to the negotiation and closing of the investment, including reasonable fees and expenses of counsel to the Investors and related due diligence expenses incurred by

the Investors. The amount of proceeds from the investment that may be used by the Company to pay for transaction fees and expenses shall be capped at 5% of the face amount of the investment, and all other transaction fees and expenses shall be paid by the principals of the Company. All transaction documents relating to the issuance of the investment shall be prepared by counsel for the Investors.

Legal Fees: Each party will bear its respective legal expenses with respect to the issuance of the Series A Preferred Shares. Counsel for the Company will be responsible for preparing the investment documents.

Governance and Control Investor Rights Term Sheet Parameters

This group of term sheet clauses defines additional rights and protections given to the preferred share investors. Giving investors some elements of control in the startup via BOD seats, voting rights on key decisions, and veto rights via protective provisions emphasizes that experienced investors should be viewed as key partners in the management of the startup, not just silent investors of cash.

Right of First Refusal on Sales by Founders and Co-Sale Rights

ALTERNATE SECTION WORDING: ROFR | CO-SALE RIGHTS

The Right of First Refusal portion of this clause says that if a founder sells his or her shares, then the preferred share investor gets the right to buy those founder shares first. Doing so results in increasing the investor's equity ownership percentage in the company.

In most cases, the startup company has the right of first refusal to buy a founder's shares. If the company doesn't want to exercise the right to buy, then the preferred share investor has the right to purchase (on a pro rata basis) the shares, at the same price proposed by the founder.

The co-sale rights portion of this clause gives the preferred share investor the right to sell shares (on a pro rata basis) alongside the founder, participating in the co-sale of shares. In other words, if the founder is "getting out", the preferred shareholder also has the right to "get out".

Example Wording

> **Right of First Refusal and Co-Sale Agreement:**
> Founders will enter into a right of first refusal and
> co-sale agreement pursuant to which any Founder
> who proposes to sell all or a portion of his/her shares
> to a third party must either permit the holders of
> the Series A Preferred shares at their option to i)
> to purchase such stock on the same terms as the
> proposed transferee, or ii) sell a proportionate part
> of their shares on the same terms offered by the
> proposed transferee. Such right will terminate upon
> the closing of an IPO.

Participation Rights

ALTERNATE SECTION WORDING: PREEMPTIVE RIGHTS | RIGHT OF FIRST
REFUSAL FOR NEW STOCK OFFERINGS

This clause says that if the startup company sells shares
to raise more money, the existing preferred shareholders
have the right to buy the new shares first, before any new
investors come into the picture.

Participation rights give existing investors the opportunity
to increase their own stake in the startup, as well as a
mechanism to control or prevent new investors from joining
equity ownership picture of the startup. More cooks in
the kitchen can often make key decision making a difficult
process, and seasoned investors like to protect their interests
by limiting the number of players that have a say in the
company.

For example, the participation clause in the term sheet might
require at least a 25% ownership on a fully diluted basis to
activate the right of first refusal (ROFR). Then, the preferred

share investor can only buy the new offering up to their pro-rata share on a fully diluted basis. The graphic below illustrates this concept.

Note that in the example below, the Series A VCs own 35% equity, thus exceeding the 25% threshold for the participation right clause, allowing them the right to buy up to their pro rata amount of the new funding offering.

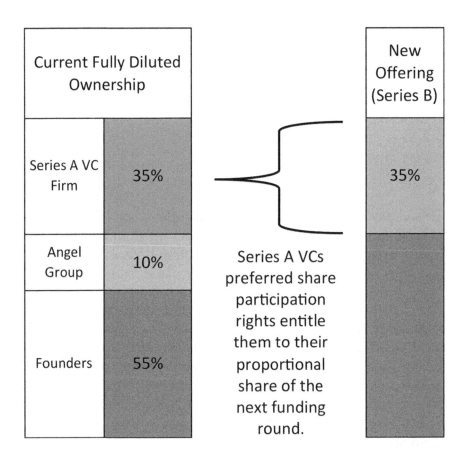

Example Wording

> **Participation Rights:** Major Purchasers (at least 25% equity on a fully diluted basis) will have the right to participate on a pro rata basis in subsequent issuances of equity securities.

Registration Rights

ALTERNATE SECTION WORDING: REGISTRATION

 This term sheet language clarifies that if the startup registers its stock on the public markets, then the startup must also register the investors stock shares and pay for the legal fees to get it done.

Registration rights clauses are common to VC level deals, with three aspects typically covered—demand registration, piggyback registration, and S-3 registration:

Demand Registration. This type of clause states that if enough of the preferred share investors agree, they have the right to force the startup to go public, registering the startup's stock on the public markets.

Example Wording

> **Demand Registration:** Beginning on the earlier of five (5) years after the initial closing, or six (6) months after the Public Offering, the holders of at least fifty-one percent (51%) of the Preferred Stock, shall be entitled to one (1) demand registration of their shares.

61

Piggyback Registration. In this variation, if the startup registers its stock on the public markets, then the startup must also register the investors' stock shares and pay the associated legal fees.

Example Wording

> **Piggyback Registration:** The Investors shall be entitled to "piggyback" registration rights on all securities registration statements of the Company, subject to the right of the Company and its underwriters to reduce (but no less than thirty percent (30%) of any offerings after the Public Offering) the number of shares proposed to be registered pro rata among the Investors and the Company's other stockholders.

S-3 Registration. Form S-3 is used to register stockholder shares with the SEC. Form S-3 is a more abbreviated registration document used after the startup has already completed the long and expensive process of registering its stock with the SEC, in preparation for an IPO.

By requiring the startup to file form S-3, preferred shares investors lay the groundwork for their shares to be included in the SEC filing process, at the startup's expense. Legal and accounting fees for SEC filing are very costly, so investors don't want to pay for registering their stock.

Because of the high registration expenses, founders should attempt to limit the number of S-3 registrations per year and set a high bar for the investment amount required to qualify for registration, say $1,000,000 or more.

Example Wording

> **S-3 Registration:** The holders of at least thirty
> percent (30%) of the Preferred Stock shall be
> entitled to unlimited demand registrations on Form
> S-3 (if available to the Company and not more
> than once every twelve (12) months) with respect
> to Common Stock issued upon conversion of the
> Preferred Stock, provided the gross proceeds
> of each registered offering are not less than
> $1,000,000.

Board Representation

ALTERNATE SECTION WORDING: BOARD COMPOSITION | BOARD SEATS

This clause states that because the preferred share investors now hold significant shares due to the investment, the preferred shared investors are entitled to name one or more representatives as board members in the startup.

The board representation clause specifies how many BOD members the preferred share investors get to elect, and sometimes stipulates the overall composition of the startup's board.

Once you establish a formal board of directors, that board controls the startup. The CEO reports to the board and can be fired by the board. This is why most founders seek to maintain full control of the BOD by maintaining a majority ownership stake in the startup, at least during the early stages of the company. If the startup goes on to raise large amount of investment cash from VCs, it's likely that some degree of control and perhaps a majority ownership will be relinquished to the large investors.

Detailed BOD issues are beyond the scope of this guide, so be sure to talk with your experienced startup lawyer and advisors on this issue.

A typical early-stage startup board of directors has three to seven members, made up of a combination of the following types of members:

- **The founders and other company executives**

- **The investors (or their designees)**

- **Independent members not affiliated with the startup or investors**

The following graphic shows how the composition of a BOD grows and changes as the startup matures.

EARLY-STAGE STARTUP BOARD	**GROWTH-STAGE** STARTUP BOARD
1. Founder (CEO)	1. Founder
2. Angel Investor	2. CEO
3. Independent	3. Series A VC
	4. Series B VC
	5. Independent

Board Observers

Early-stage equity investment deals such as first round angel deals, often don't require a full BOD member to represent the preferred share investor(s). Instead, a board observer member named by the preferred share investor attends the board meetings. The board observer can ask limited questions but does not have a vote in any board decisions.

Example Wordings

Board Seats: One (1) director elected by holders of a majority of common stock, one (1) elected by holders of a majority of Series Seed and one (1) elected by mutual consent.

Board Composition: The Company's board of directors shall be comprised of three (3) individuals with one (1) representative being the CEO of the Company, one (1) representative being the Lead Investors or his designee (the Series A Director), and one (1) representative being an individual mutually agreed upon by the Lead Investor and the CEO of the Company.

Voting Rights

The Voting Rights section defines how the preferred share investors get to vote within the company's decision making process. Generally, the language states that the preferred share investors get to vote on anything that the founders can vote on.

Examples of key voting rights items include:

- Changes to the articles of incorporation

- Changes to the corporate bylaws

- Changes to the size of the board of directors

- Employee salary levels (including founder salaries)

- Raising additional capital or debt

- Liquidation or dissolution of the corporation

Example Wording

> **Voting Rights:** The Series A Preferred shall vote together with the Common Stock on an as-converted basis, and not as a separate class, except (i) [so long as [insert fixed number, or %, or "any"] shares of Series A Preferred are outstanding,] the Series A Preferred as a class shall be entitled to elect [_____] [(_)] members of the Board (the "Series A Directors"), and (ii) as required by law. The Company's Certificate of Incorporation will provide that the number of authorized shares of Common Stock may be increased or decreased with the approval of a majority of the Preferred and Common Stock, voting together as a single class, and without a separate class vote by the Common Stock.

66

Voting Rights: Except as required by law or as otherwise set forth herein, the holders of the Preferred Stock will vote on an as-converted to Common Stock basis on all matters on which holders of the Common Stock are entitled to vote.

Information Rights

ALTERNATE SECTION WORDING: INFORMATION | INVESTOR UPDATES

In this section, the founders agree to provide status reports and financial performance information about the company to investors several times per year.

The Information rights section defines what information and reports are required and the reporting schedule, and sometimes which investors are entitled to receive the information. For example, it might state that all investors get the right to receive the information, or only preferred share investors, or only preferred share investors who own more than a specific percentage of stock.

It's a benefit to founders to limit the number of investors who will receive reports and financials. Many startups have sensitive or proprietary information, so it makes sense to keep the distribution list small.

Financial Reports. The standard set of financial reports that investors require include *profit and loss (P&L) statements, balance sheets, and cash flow statements.* Once the startup has set up a simple accounting system and established a process for diligently feeding the accounting system (issuing purchase orders, tracking credit card transactions in detail, logging bank deposits, transfers, and withdrawals, etc.), generating the standard reports is a matter of a few clicks.

In addition to running the financial reports, it's a good idea to "package" the information going to the investors.

Including a written summary of the financial highlights and headline developments is good practice. Also, founders should call attention to out of the norm occurrences such as one-time or unexpected expenses and any changes to the accounting process.

Audited or Unaudited Financials. As you will read in the example wording for an information rights clause below, some investors require the financial reports to be audited. This means the startup must hire an outside accounting firm to audit the financial systems and sign off that the information in the reports is accurate, to the best of their professional ability. Paying the accountants for an audit can be expensive and time consuming. Founders should attempt to limit any audit requirements to once per year at a maximum.

Operating Plans and Forward Looking Financial Forecasts. For a startup that is up and running, founders should recast the business plan as an operating plan that clearly outlines the key milestones the team intends to achieve. Typical milestones for a growing startup include sales goals, new product introductions, new customer segment plans, and team expansion. Investors want to know about these plans and the associated budget and resulting revenue forecasts. The information rights terms enable preferred share investors to secure the flow of this kind of information.

How often should the information be provided? The information rights wording also states how often the startup must deliver the various reports—yearly, quarterly, monthly, and so on. Obviously, founder-favorable wording limits the reporting frequency.

The following figure shows a typical timeline for the flow of information to investors. Investors and founders typically engage in much more frequent contact.

INFORMATION RIGHTS TIMELINE

Jan	Feb	Mar	Apr	May	Jun	Jul	Aug	Sep	Oct	Nov	Dec	Jan	Feb	Mar
(i)			$			$			$			(i)		($)

(i) – Operating plans and financial forecasts due each year

$ – Unaudited financial reports due to investors each quarter

($) – Audited financial reports due 90 days after year end

Example Wordings

Information Rights: The Company will deliver to shareholders:

Audited financial statements or reviewed (as determined by investors) for each fiscal year within 90 days after the end of the fiscal year and management-prepared quarterly financial statements for the first three quarters of the year within 30 days after the end of each quarter.

Annual budgets at least 30 days prior to the beginning of each fiscal year.

Quarterly updates on progress and accomplishments and anticipated progress against target in next period.

Notification of any material defaults or litigation and any other information reasonably requested.

The investor also will have standard inspection and visitation rights.

Information Rights: The Company shall deliver customary audited annual, unaudited quarterly and monthly financial statements and budgets to each Investor who purchases at least ____ shares of Series A Preferred (a "*Major Investor*"). Each Investor shall also be entitled to standard inspection and visitation rights.

Drag Along Rights

 Drag along rights give the investor the right to force the common shareholders (founders, key employees, and any others) and any minority preferred shareholders to agree/vote to sell the startup. Drag along rights are common in VC deals.

There are two primary reasons for a drag along rights clause, as follows:

1. We want out. Investors want to get out of the investment and sell or merge the startup with another company. In this case, the startup is probably performing OK but not meeting the investor's high hopes. The drag along rights clause gives the investor the ability to force the sale of the company to perhaps recouping the investment.

2. Little guys must abide. As a more benign goal, drag along rights help prevents a small number of stockholders, or small percentage holder, from holding up the sale of the startup. If the majority of investors and the founders want to move ahead with a sale of the startup, they don't have to get all of the small shareholders approval to act.

This graphic illustrates the influence a drag along provision can have over founders and even other minority preferred shareholders.

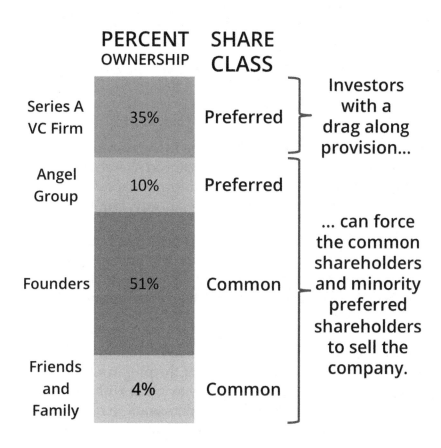

	PERCENT OWNERSHIP	SHARE CLASS	
Series A VC Firm	35%	Preferred	Investors with a drag along provision...
Angel Group	10%	Preferred	... can force the common shareholders and minority preferred shareholders to sell the company.
Founders	51%	Common	
Friends and Family	4%	Common	

Example Wording

> **Drag Along Rights:** The holders of the Common or Preferred Stock shall enter into a drag-along agreement whereby if a majority of the holders of Series A Preferred Stock agree to a sale or liquidation of the Company, the holders of the remaining Preferred and Common Stock shall consent to and raise no objections to such sale

Protective Provisions

Protective provisions state that if the founders want to take any action that might affect preferred shareholders' investments, the founders have to inform the preferred shareholders and get their collective approval first.

The protective provision section of a term sheet outlines several conditions under which founders must get preferred share investor approval. Protective provisions give the preferred share investors veto rights over decisions that would harm their investment.

Typical wording in protective provisions sections require the written consent of at least 51% of the preferred share investors before founders can move forward with the issue or change. For example, if the founders want to raise more money by issuing more stock, the existing preferred share investors must agree in writing.

Here's a list of common protective provisions:

- Merge, sell, or liquidate the company, or any other transaction that results in a change of control of the company.

- Change the capitalization structure of the company, such as authorize the creation of additional stock shares or new classes of shares.

- Issue stock senior to or equal to the stock held by the preferred share investor(s).

- Change the certificate of incorporation or bylaws.

- Change the composition or size of the board of directors.

- Pay or declare dividends.

- Buy back any common stock.

- Take on a debt obligation such as a loan.

Example Wording.

Protective Provisions: [So long as [insert fixed number, or %, or "any"] shares of Series A Preferred are outstanding,] in addition to any other vote or approval required under the Company's Charter or Bylaws, the Company will not, without the written consent of the holders of at least [___]% of the Company's Series A Preferred, either directly or by amendment, merger, consolidation, or otherwise:

(i) liquidate, dissolve or wind up the affairs of the Company, or effect any merger or consolidation or any other Deemed Liquidation Event; (ii) amend, alter, or repeal any provision of the Certificate of Incorporation or Bylaws [in a manner adverse to the Series A Preferred];(iii) create or authorize the creation of or issue any other security convertible into or exercisable for any equity security, having rights, preferences or privileges senior to or on parity with the Series A Preferred, or increase the authorized number of shares of Series A Preferred; (iv) purchase or redeem or pay any dividend on any capital stock prior to the Series A Preferred, [other than stock repurchased from former employees or consultants in connection with the cessation of their employment/services, at the lower of fair market value or cost;] [other than as approved by the Board, including the approval of [_____] Series A Director(s)]; or (v) create or authorize the creation of any debt security [if the Company's aggregate indebtedness would exceed $[_____][other than equipment leases or bank lines of credit][unless such debt security has received the prior approval of the Board of Directors, including the approval of [_____] Series A Director(s)]; (vi) create or hold capital stock in any subsidiary that is not a wholly-owned subsidiary or dispose of any subsidiary stock or all or substantially all of any subsidiary assets; [or (vii) increase or decrease the size of the Board of Directors].

Pari Passu

Pari passu is a Latin phrase meaning *in equal step*, or on equal footing and without preference. This term is most often seen in VC-level investment term sheets. The pari passu clause basically states that if the startup issues any new classes of stock, such as a Series B round, that new stock shall have equal rights with prior classes (Series A, for example) in terms of liquidation preferences, voting rights, and so on. In other words, the term prohibits the founders from creating a new class of stock that puts existing investors second in line.

If the startup raises several rounds of equity funding, it's likely that different sets of investors might attempt to negotiate seniority of their preferred shares over previous preferred share investors. For example, consider a liquidation preference of a Series B investor that makes the Series B Preferred senior over any Series A investor's preferences. With this ranking, the Series B investor would get liquidation proceeds from an acquisition before any Series A investors get any proceeds. The pari passu clause attempts to uncomplicate such rankings by keeping all the preferred shareholders on equal footing, dividing the proceeds based on the proportion of shares owned.

 Last Money In Rules. The above being said, a common phrase in startup investing is "the last money in rules." In other words, whoever puts in the most recent funding calls all the shots. Earlier investors are urged to agree with any new arrangements (such as getting diluted, allowing seniority in liquidation, etc.). If the existing investors don't go along with the new conditions, the new money investor might back out, and the viability of the startup is put in jeopardy due to lack of funding.

Example Wording

Pari Passu: Except as set forth, the Preferred Stock will be treated as pari passu with the Series A Preferred of the Company (the "prior Preferred" with the Preferred and Prior Preferred collectively referred to as Series Preferred).

Exclusivity

 The exclusivity section seeks to prevent the founders from initiating and working funding deals with other investors for some period of time.

A 30-day duration is typical for most exclusivity clauses. Any longer timeframe proposes is considered unreasonable, and founders should push back on the investors asking for the nonstandard exclusivity duration.

Most angel investor term sheets do not ask for exclusivity, because founders are usually pitching multiple angels at one time. Plus, angel level deals are often syndicated among a few or even several angel groups, so exclusivity is counter productive.

For VC level deals the amount of funding is much larger and VCs often compete against one another to get the most attractive deals. In this case, exclusivity makes more sense. The VCs will attempt to limit founders from shopping around. Or they might request that the founders at least give the VCs visibility of any other proposed deals, allowing the VCs the option to match any third party deals.

From the VC perspective, it's reasonable to ask the founders to be committed to the deal discussions with the investors that have put forth the current term sheet. This assumes the founders will not shop around for additional investors and play one against the other.

Example Wording

> **Exclusivity:** Neither the Company nor any of the Company's directors, officers, employees, agents or representatives will solicit, encourage, or entertain proposals from or enter into negotiations with or furnish any nonpublic information to any other person or entity regarding the possible sale of the Company's stock. The Company shall notify the Investors promptly of any proposals by third parties with respect to the acquisition of the Company's stock and furnish the Investors the material terms thereof. The Company shall deal exclusively with the Investors with respect to any such possible transaction and Investors shall have the right to match such proposed transactions in lieu of such third parties. This right shall last for a period of 30 days from the date hereof.

Confidentiality

Tied closely to the idea of exclusivity is the confidentiality clause. The investors do not want the founders to reveal any deal terms or other information to competing investors.

Example Wording

> **Confidentiality:** The existence and terms of this Term Sheet, and the fact that negotiations may be ongoing with the Investors, are strictly confidential and may not be disclosed to anyone except the Company's directors, executive officers, and legal counsel.

Conditions of Financing

ALTERNATE SECTION WORDING: PRECEDENTS OF FINANCING | ADDITIONAL CONDITIONS | CONDITIONS OF CLOSING

This section of the term sheet includes several items that the investor requires the startup to complete prior to closing of the funding deal. Often part of the "deferred housekeeping" that founders put off until they are forced to, this section requires founders to formalize items such as employment and non-compete agreements with the startup, legal assignment of all inventions and other intellectual property to the startup entity, and establishing key man insurance policies.

An experienced startup legal firm will have boilerplate agreements that cover all of these common startup housekeeping tasks.

Founder Vesting and Restricted Stock

Many startups choose to structure the founder shares as restricted stock, using a *restricted stock purchase agreement (RSPA)*.

Under an RSPA, some or all of each founder's shares are reserved or "taken away," and "earned" back over time, known as *vesting*. The longer the vesting schedule progresses, the more shares the founder earns back. The restricted shares are assigned to the corporation, so no other person owns them. If the founder leaves the startup before his or her restricted shares vest, the startup corporation can use th shares to recruit other talent.

Vesting founders' stock provides investors some level of assurance that founders have an incentive to follow through. This approach also protects the founders from each other

78

and creates an incentive to stay engaged in the company.

Example Wording

> **Founder Vesting:** Each Key Holder shall have four years vesting beginning [_____]. Full acceleration upon "Double Trigger."

Insurance

Many early-stage startups are brought to life by the vision and passion of a single founder. Over time, this founder attracts co-founders and other key employees to help transform the vision and idea into something tangible that customers or users love. In many cases, the loss of the visionary founder kills the startup entirely. Investors mitigate this risk by requiring the startup to secure a key man life insurance policy. If the key man dies, the investor has some chance of recouping a portion of his investment via the insurance policy.

Example Wording

> **Key Man Insurance:** The Company will have obtained "key man" life insurance on the lives of [*Your Name Here*] in an amount not less than $1,000,000, naming the Company as beneficiary.

Founder Employment Agreements

Dealing with paperwork such as employment letters and non-compete agreements usually ranks last on a founder's to-do list. But from the investor's perspective, requiring the each founder to sign a formal employment agreement between the founder and startup corporation gives investors another assurance that the proper corporate housekeeping is getting done. Additionally, investors don't want a founder leaving the company and starting a competing company. Non-compete and non-disclosure provisions in the employment contract helps reduce this possibility.

Example Wording

> **Employment and Non-Compete Agreements:** As a condition to the Investment, the Founders must have entered into a binding Employment Agreement with the Company, with non-compete provisions.

Invention Assignment

For many startups, *intellectual property (IP)* is the company's most valuable asset. Because many founders create key aspects of the startup's IP before incorporation, investors want to make sure that the rights to the assets (code, prototypes, designs, process diagrams, and trademarks) are assigned to the company. As part of the due diligence of the investment process and term sheet requirements, founders will have to show signed invention assignments to the investors.

Example Wording

> **Invention Assignment:** Each Key Holder shall have assigned all relevant IP to the Company before closing.

Thank You

This concludes the *Founder's Pocket Guide: Term Sheets and Preferred Shares.*

We hope you find our content and supporting tools useful for your startup journey.

We are always looking for feedback on our startup tools. If you have comments, feedback, or corrections, please send us a note.

info@1x1media.com

http://www.1x1media.com

#